MW00861500

Entangled Butterflies

COLORING BOOK

Angela Porter

DOVER PUBLICATIONS, INC.
MINEOLA, NEW YORK

These thirty-one lovely full-page butterfly illustrations feature nature's beauties against complex backgrounds that will come to life with the inspired touch of the experienced colorist. These lively and delicate creatures float and flutter among stars, flowers, and many other glorious natural wonders. Pages are perforated and printed on one side only for easy removal and display.

Copyright

Copyright © 2018 by Angela Porter
All rights reserved.

Bibliographical Note

Entangled Butterflies Coloring Book is a new work, first published by Dover Publications, Inc., in 2018.

International Standard Book Number

ISBN-13: 978-0-486-82814-5
ISBN-10: 0-486-82814-X

Manufactured in the United States by LSC Communications
82814X03   2019
www.doverpublications.com